Highlights

501

BACKYARD ANIMAL JOKE-TIVITIES

Riddles, Puzzles, Fun Facts, Cartoons, Tongue Twisters, and Other Giggles!

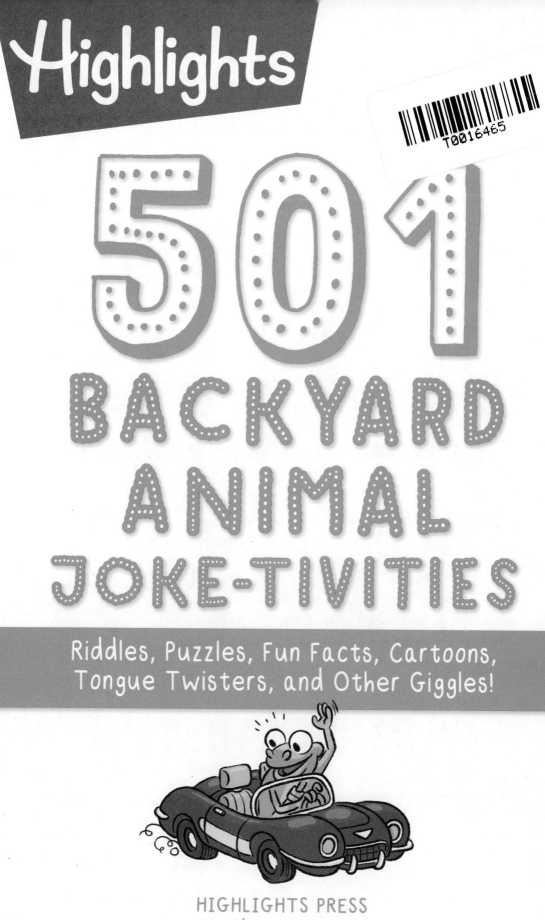

HIGHLIGHTS PRESS
Honesdale, Pennsylvania

WHICH CRITTERS FIT?

Draw the missing animals in the blank spaces so each animal appears only once in each row and column.

Try to say these

TONGUE TWISTERS

three times, fast.

Daring deer don't dawdle.

Duncan Duck ducks dodgeballs.

The squirrel squished squash.

Six snakes slithered slowly.

GOING WITH THE FLOW

It's a nice day to relax by the river. Without clues or knowing what to look for, can you find the **18** objects hidden in this scene?

What animals can jump higher than a house?

All of them. Houses can't jump.

TIC TAC ROW

Each of these birds has something in common with the other two birds in the same row—across, down, and diagonally. For example, in the top row across, each bird is blue. Can you tell what's alike in each row?

Try to say these
TONGUE TWISTERS
three times, fast.

Five finches find figs.   **The cardinal chirps cheerfully.**

KIDS' SCIENCE QUESTIONS

Why do cardinals hit their beaks on glass doors?

Some birds, such as cardinals and robins, may attack their own reflections in glass windows or doors. These birds claim a home area and protect it by chasing away other birds. When a cardinal or robin sees its own reflection, the bird may think the reflection is another bird and peck at the window to chase away the "intruder."

We don't know of a trick that always makes birds stop pecking at their reflections. Some people tape a sheet of white paper on the inside of the window to reduce the reflection. Others have tried putting up a cutout that looks like the shadow of a falcon or some other enemy of the pecking bird. Maybe you'll find the perfect solution.

The feathers that cover and protect our ears are called auricular feathers.

Do birds have ears?

Yes, birds have ears. It's difficult to see the ears on most birds because they are covered by feathers, but many birds have an excellent sense of hearing.

What do you call somebody who steals birds?

A bird-ler

What is a rabbit's favorite game?
Hopscotch

Where do rabbits go after they get married?
On a bunnymoon

How does a rabbit keep its fur neat?
It uses a hare-brush.

What do you get when you cross a rabbit and a frog?
A bunny ribbit

How do you know that carrots are good for your eyes?
Have you ever seen a rabbit wearing glasses?

KIDS' SCIENCE QUESTIONS

How many teeth does a rabbit have?

A rabbit has 28 teeth in all. Six of these are front teeth. The rest are in the back of the mouth. A rabbit's teeth never stop growing. In fact, they can grow around three or four inches a year! To prevent its chompers from getting too long, a rabbit chews on rough plants, twigs, and tree branches. This wears the teeth down and keeps them short.

GARDENING TIME

Can you find at least **20** differences between these two pictures?

LEADER OF THE PACK

Wolf down these facts about wolves. Then find the **15** objects hidden in this scene.

The average gray wolf can be 36 to 63 inches long and weigh between 40 and 175 pounds.

Wolves can run about 5 miles per hour, but they can sprint as fast as 35 miles per hour.

Wolves don't eat every day, because they can't always find food. So when wolves catch a large animal, they stuff themselves with as much as 20 pounds of meat in one meal.

The most common wolf species is the gray wolf. Gray wolves aren't only gray. Their fur can also be black, white, or brown.

Wolves mostly eat large animals with hooves, such as deer and moose.

Wolves have sharp senses of hearing and smell. They're also good at running, climbing, and swimming.

The average life span of a wolf is 6 to 8 years.

Huskies are a type of dog that looks like a wolf. Many people think that huskies are part wolf, but huskies are 100 percent dog.

WILD ABOUT NUTS

These squirrels are on the hunt! Follow the paths to see who gets each nut.

FUN FACT

A squirrel's ankles can turn almost all the way around. That way, the squirrel can dig its claws into the bark of a tree and climb down headfirst.

MY FAVORITE SEASON

The leaves know it's autumn.
They're falling today.
The geese know it's autumn.
They're flying away.
I know it's autumn.
I love it!
I'll stay.

WHAT'S WRONG?

Which things in this picture are silly? It's up to you!

Why is the
sky so high?
....
So birds don't hit
their heads

Bee... "B-E-E." Bee.

What did one worm say to the other worm?
"Where on earth have you been?"

Why did the squirrel take so long to eat the walnut?
It was a tough nut to crack.

What's smarter than a talking bird?
A spelling bee

Where do squirrels go to school before kindergarten?
Tree school

Knock, knock.
Who's there?
Bunny.
Bunny who?
Any-bunny think this is funny?

What did the round bunny say to the square bunny?
"You're not from a round hare, are you?"

What is the rudest bird?
A mockingbird

What's worse than finding a worm in your apple?
Finding two worms in your apple.

Hoot! Hoot!

Hoot! Hoot!

WHAT'S THE BUZZ?

We don't mean to bug you. But we do want you to search for the **35** insects hiding in this grid. Look for them up, down, across, and diagonally. How many can you spot?

WORD LIST

~~APHID~~
BEDBUG
BEETLE
BLOWFLY
BUTTERFLY
CICADA
COCKROACH
CRICKET
DRAGONFLY
EARWIG
FIRE ANT
FIREFLY
FLEA
FRUIT FLY
GNAT
GRASSHOPPER
HONEYBEE
HORNET
HOUSEFLY
KATYDID
LADYBUG
LEAFHOPPER
LOCUST
LOUSE
MANTIS
MAYFLY
MEALYBUG
MIDGE
MOSQUITO
MOTH
SILVERFISH
STINKBUG
TERMITE
WALKING STICK
WEEVIL

What type of vegetable do bugs hate?
. . . .
Squash

Which bug never does its chores?
. . . .
A lazy-bug

14

```
T E F R U I T F L Y Y L F E R I F
E E B U Z Z T S I L V E R F I S H
R B M N E T M E A L Y B U G O X K
M Y N Y S A L J N C R I C K E T L
I E U U U C O C K R O A C H F G E
T N C L O D D R A G O N F L Y U A
E O F Y L F W O L B R H K P G B F
L H B G U B K N I T S V A H K Y H
E B E D B U G X A W Y U T O W D O
K L Y M B U T T E R F L Y U H A P
M A Y F L Y A V L S R X D S I L P
P D R O N E N V F M X V I E R E E
W A L K I N G S T I C K D F R O R
E W E E V I L E A N V I J L U T S
C A P H E E L G H C M S C Y G P I
H P R C V T D T O F I R E A N T T
I H X W E V O E G D I M D U D V N
R I T E I M O S Q U I T O H N A A
P D B Y P G R A S S H O P P E R M
```

SKUNKY SCENTS FOR SALE

Everyone can find the perfect scent at this store!
Can you find the objects hidden in this scene?

How much money does a skunk have?
· · · · · · · · · · ·
One scent

candle

saltshaker

baseball

ring

glove

dog dish

butterfly

fish

seashell

ruler

banana

needle

saucepan

screwdriver

golf club

KIDS' SCIENCE QUESTIONS

Why do skunks spray at you when you come near them?

The skunk's spray is its way of protecting itself. All small animals have the same problem: other animals may try to eat them. Birds can fly to safety, porcupines can curl up with their sharp quills sticking out, and skunks can spray a musk that has a very unpleasant smell.

None of these defenses are perfect. Some animals can get around the porcupine's quills. Birds can be caught by cats and by bigger birds. And some owls don't seem to be bothered at all by the skunk's smell.

If you get sprayed by a skunk, is tomato juice the solution?

Don't try this solution unless you have the help of an adult! Do not get this mixture near your eyes or mouth.

Tomato juice can help mask the smell, but it can't remove the odor. The smelliest part of a skunk's spray comes from sulfur compounds called thiols. The best way to get rid of the smell is to chemically change the *thiols*. A mixture of water, hydrogen peroxide, and baking soda creates oxygen, which combines with the thiols to "de-smell" them. And since skunk spray is oily, adding detergent to the mixture helps because detergents break up and remove oils.

BAKING SODA

TOMATO JUICE

LAUGHING LIZARDS

Welcome to the Lizard Lounge! To figure out the punch line to the riddle this lizard is telling, use the clues below to find out what letter goes in each numbered space. Enjoy the show!

1. This letter is with some flowers.
2. Look on the piano for this letter.
3. You'll find this letter with some meatballs.
4. This letter is on a stage light.
5. This letter is on a waiter's tray.
6. Look on someone's shoe for this letter.
7. You'll find this letter on a stool.
8. Someone is wearing this letter as a necklace.
9. This letter is hanging on the curtains.

What do you get if you mix a rabbit and a snake?

___ ___ ___ ___ ___ ___ ___ ___ ___
5   9   3   8   1   6   2   7   4

Do ducks swim underwater?

Some ducks swim underwater, others don't. The ones that swim underwater are known as diving ducks. These birds plunge down to look for food like shrimp and fish. The long-tailed duck is one of the deepest divers. Swimming with its wings, it can travel 200 feet under the water's surface. Ducks that mostly stay above water are called dabbling ducks. When they're hungry, they look for seeds on the shore and insects at shallow depths.

Why do ducklings follow their mothers?

The moment a duckling opens its eyes, it learns to recognize its mom and siblings. It's almost as if images of the family are stamped in the duckling's mind. This is called *imprinting*. The duckling can tell its family apart from other ducks, and by instinct, it follows its mom wherever she goes. It's important for ducklings to recognize and stick close to their families. This makes it less likely that they'll wander off into danger.

DOUBLE DUCKS

Can you find at least **11** differences between these two pictures?

BONUS
How many D's can you find?

HELP THE CARTOONISTS!

These cartoons are missing their captions. Write your own punch lines, then check out the cartoonists' original gags on page 136.

BEAR-TISTS

These bears are crafty! Can you find the objects hidden in this scene?

What do you call a bear with no teeth?

. . . .

A gummy bear

banana

worm

piece of cake

book

tack

candle

mallet

spoon

SNOW-TUNNEL MAZE

Which animal can find a cozy place to sleep?
Follow the paths to figure out which animal makes it to the bed.

FINISH

LAUGH ATTACK

Why were the bears cold, even under their warmest quilt?

They slept in their bear skin.

Why did the bee go south for the winter?

To visit an ant in Florida

What do you call a bird that stays up north all winter?

A brrrd

What is a turtle's favorite thing to wear in the winter?

A turtleneck

KIDS' SCIENCE QUESTIONS

Why do some animals leave in winter to go someplace warm?

When weather turns cold, humans can turn up the furnace and find food at a grocery store. But what can animals do? Many of them can't find their usual foods when it's cold. Plants die off or stop growing leaves and fruit. Animals they might prey on leave for warmer climates or snuggle down in dens.

Animals solve these problems with one of two basic strategies. Either they have bodies and diets adapted to colder climates—or they go somewhere warmer.

Come south with me!

SQUIRRELS store nuts to eat when foods are scarce.

BEARS eat lots of food in the fall, giving them fat to live on as they go into light hibernation.

BIRDS with wings capable of long flight leave to find food in warmer climates.

RED FOXES will eat different foods, depending on what's available.

I stay put, even when it's cold!

I say just sleep through it.

I can't. I'd get too hungry.

CHOIR ON THE WIRES

It's time for the birds' daily concert! Can you find the objects hidden in this scene?

BONUS!
Can you find the dinosaur, saltshaker, paper clip, and horseshoe?

open book

canoe

banana

ruler

piece of popcorn

heart

golf club

slice of pizza

drinking straw

pennant

glove

carrot

waffle

shorts

sailboat

crescent moon

EARLY BIRDSONG

Bird out the window
sings so sweet
with a *titter* and a *chitter*
and a *tweet, tweet, tweet*.
She serenades sunrise
with each *chirp* and *cheep*.

If only she'd sing
when I'm not
trying to
sleep!

Try to say these

TONGUE TWISTERS

three times, fast.

Big birds buy buns.

The blue bluebird blinks.

Pudgy pigeons pick pretty posies.

Gray geese graze in the green grass.

RIDDLE SUDOKU

Fill in the squares so that the six letters appear only once in each row, column, and 2 x 3 box. Then read the orange squares to find out the answer to the riddle.

Our Sudoku puzzles use letters instead of numbers.

Riddle:

What did the nut say when it sneezed?

LETTERS: **A C E H S W**

	W		S	A	
S			E		
H			W		
	O	A			
		W			S
E	S	C		H	

Answer:

"___ ___ ___ ___ ___!"

WHAT'S WRONG?

Which things in this picture are silly? It's up to you!

WALNUTS

CASHEWS

What is a squirrel's favorite instrument?

The acorn-dion

29

BAT-TING ORDER

More than 900 kinds of bats live in the world. Thirty-five are hiding in this grid. How many can you find? Look up, down, across, backward, and diagonally. When you're done, search the leftover letters for more bats. If you can find all **13** extra **BAT**s, you've got a perfect batting average.

WORD LIST

BIG-EARED
BONNETED
BROWN
BUMBLEBEE
CAVE
COLONIAL
DAWN
EASTERN RED
EVENING
FREE-TAILED
FRINGED
GHOST-FACED
GOLDEN
GRAY
HOARY
HORSESHOE
INDIANA
KEEN'S

LEAF-NOSED
LONG-EARED
LONG-NOSED
MASTIFF
NECTAR
PALLID
SMALL-FOOTED
SMOKY
SOUTHEASTERN
SOUTHERN YELLOW
SPOTTED
TRI-COLORED
VAMPIRE
VESPER
WESTERN RED
WOOLLY
WRINKLE-FACED

What do bats do for exercise?

Acro-bat-ics

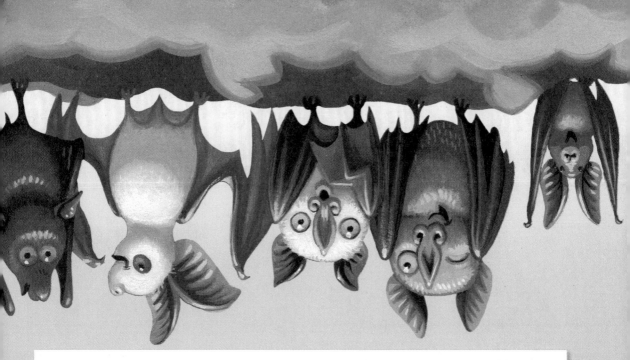

```
L O N G N O S E D A B A T Q X R B
B A T W S M A L L F O O T E D E A
I N D I A N A (B I G E A R E D) P T
S C I L T D A R N D E T T O P S E
O C O L O N I A L B A T N S A E O
U T R I C O L O R E D R T B A V H
T A G H O S T F A C E D A S B D S
H V A M P I R E A T E T T A E B E
E T N B A T T S S L W E N T A D S
R K E E N S M A I B R T E T A E R
N Y D A T O E A A N I N C A P R O
Y B L A K H T T R B N B T T A A H
E A O Y T E B E A O K T A F L E W
L T G U E A D T B T L G R F L G O
L G O R G N I N E V E R A I I N O
O S F B B A T E C H F A B T D O L
W E S T E R N R E D A Y A S C L L
L E A F N O S E D B C Y R A O H Y
B U M B L E B E E A E B V M B A T
B D F R I N G E D T D E B R O W N
```

TIC TAC ROW

Each of these frogs has something in common with the other two frogs in the same row—across, down, and diagonally. For example, in the top row across, each frog has stripes. Can you tell what's alike in each row?

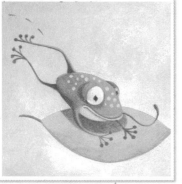

Try to say these

TONGUE TWISTERS

three times, fast.

Four freckled frogs fried french flies.

Frankie's fabulous frog ate frozen fly fondue.

FROG ON THE GO

Use the clues to find the five letters that answer the riddle.

1. The first letter is in *sheep*, but not in *sleepy*.

2. The second letter is in *owl*, but not in *wild*.

3. The third letter is in *pig*, *wasp*, and *puppy*.

4. The fourth letter is in *fish*, but not in *shelf*.

5. The fifth letter is in *hen*, *panda*, and *lion*.

What do you say to a frog who needs a ride?

" __ __ __ __ __!"

FUN FACT

A group of frogs is called an army.

33

A COOL TREAT

To find the answer to the riddle below, first cross out all the pairs of matching letters. Then write the remaining letters in order in the spaces beneath the riddle.

TT	BB	CC	AA	TH	PP	QQ
SS	EY	LL	XX	HA	KK	VV
VE	YY	DD	OO	BB	HA	GG
MM	RE	FF	EE	LL	II	CO
BB	QQ	AA	SS	ND	RR	ZZ
IT	CC	HH	PP	UU	IO	JJ
II	NI	XX	LL	RR	NG	WW

Why don't rabbits get hot in the summertime?

_ _ _ _ _   _ _ _ _ _

_ _ _ _ - _ _ _ _ _ _ _ _ _ _ _

Why Do Rabbits Have Such Long Ears?

Rabbits use their big ears to pick up the soft sounds of cats, hawks, and other animals that try to eat them. But their ears also help rabbits stay cool in hot weather. Their ears have lots of blood vessels and thin skin. When a rabbit's body gets hot, more blood flows into its ears. There, heat flows out, going through the skin and into the air. So rabbit ears are natural air conditioners!

My ears keep me cool!

LAUGH ATTACK

How do you tell old rabbits from young rabbits?
Look for the gray hares.

Why was the rabbit so happy?
She was a hop-timist.

How do rabbits go on vacation?
They take a hare-plane.

What's a rabbit's favorite dance style?
Hip-hop

What do ambitious young rabbits want to be when they grow up?
Millionhares

COME OUT OF YOUR SHELL

Stick your neck out—like this box turtle—and learn about these creatures.
Then find the **15** objects hidden in this scene.

They are called "box turtles" because the bottom part of their shell is hinged. It can close up tightly when the turtle pulls in its head.

The markings on their shells can be yellow or orange, and they can have three or four toes on their back feet.

Box turtles live near streams and ponds.

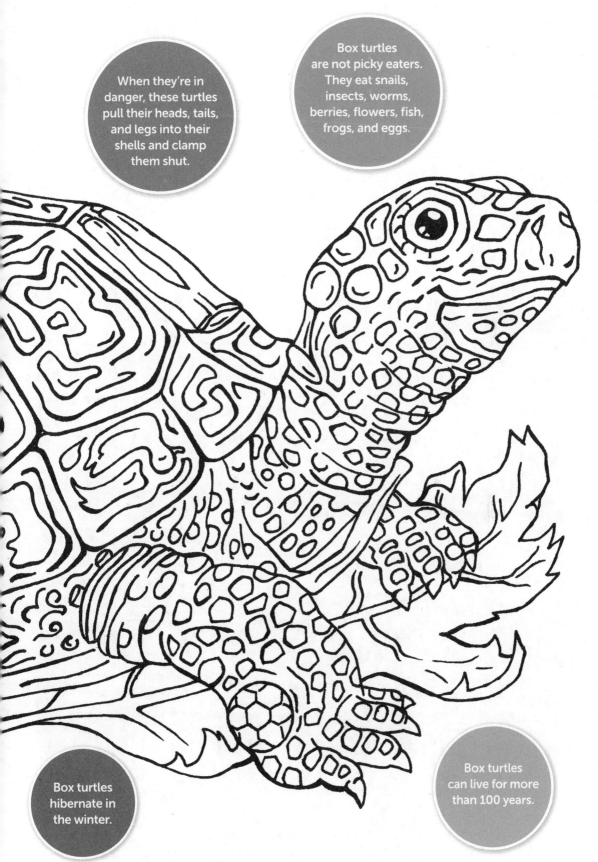

When they're in danger, these turtles pull their heads, tails, and legs into their shells and clamp them shut.

Box turtles are not picky eaters. They eat snails, insects, worms, berries, flowers, fish, frogs, and eggs.

Box turtles hibernate in the winter.

Box turtles can live for more than 100 years.

MOOSE PALS

Help Mort take the right path to find Murray.
The symbols tell him which way to move.

MOOSE MUNCH

What do you call a moose's facial hair?
. . . .
A moose-stache

When moose go meandering in the marshy muck,
I wonder if their feet ever get stuck.
Do moose mind getting muddy
as they munch tender shoots?
I may be mistaken, but I think
they might need boots!

How many M's can you find?

Try to say these

TONGUE TWISTERS

three times, fast.

Many moose munch much mush.

If goose goes to geese, do two moose make meese?

SCRAMBLED BIRDS

Why do hummingbirds hum? To find out the answer to this riddle, unscramble the bird names below. Then write the numbered letters in the spaces at the bottom of the page.

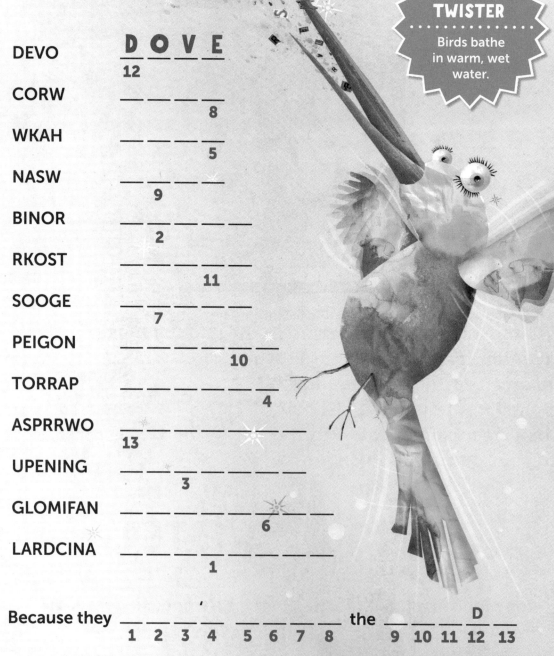

DEVO   D O V E
       12

CORW   _ _ _ _
           8

WKAH   _ _ _ _
           5

NASW   _ _ _ _
      9

BINOR   _ _ _ _ _
      2

RKOST   _ _ _ _ _
          11

SOOGE   _ _ _ _ _
      7

PEIGON   _ _ _ _ _ _
          10

TORRAP   _ _ _ _ _ _
           4

ASPRRWO   _ _ _ _ _ _ _
  13

UPENING   _ _ _ _ _ _ _
     3

GLOMIFAN   _ _ _ _ _ _ _ _
         6

LARDCINA   _ _ _ _ _ _ _ _
     1

Because they _ _ _ _ ' _ _ _ _ the _ _ _ D _ _
          1 2 3 4   5 6 7 8   9 10 11 12 13

How fast can hummingbirds fly?

The tiny hummingbird is a giant among fliers. With wings that move so fast they hum and blur, it zips from one food source to another to fuel its speed.

It can fly in all directions, even backward and upside down.

It can also hover like a helicopter. Considering the bird's size, its large brain and heart and impressive speed outshine those of many other birds and mammals.

In just one second, it can fly a few hundred times the length of its body. That would be like you running a few football fields in one second. On average, hummingbirds can fly about 30mph. Speedy, right?

A hummingbird's long tongue can reach nectar that is deep within a flower.

Its tongue has a forked tip that grabs more nectar with each lick than an unforked tongue could get.

Each wing moves in a figure 8, beating 70 to 80 times a second.

A hummingbird's iridescent colors can vary because tiny structures on the feathers reflect light differently at different angles.

Its tiny feet grip branches as it rests, but it doesn't walk much.

WHAT'S WRONG?

Which things in this picture are silly? It's up to you!

What is an owl's favorite soft drink?

Hoot beer

43

FLYING SOLO

All the butterflies but one look exactly alike. Can you find the one unique butterfly?

Who is
the king of
the insects?
· · · · · · · · · · ·
The monarch
butterfly

KIDS' SCIENCE QUESTIONS

Why do monarch butterflies migrate in the fall?

Unlike many North American insects, monarch butterflies cannot survive freezing temperatures. So, at the end of each summer, monarchs set out on a long journey south. The migrating butterflies fly about 30 miles each day, facing such dangers as storms, extreme temperatures, and collisions with moving vehicles.

By late October, millions of monarchs arrive in California and Mexico to spend the winter. Some will have flown almost 3,000 miles! But these tough travelers are built to make the journey.

Monarchs soar and glide on air currents instead of always flapping their wings. This saves energy and keeps the wings in good shape.

By day, they travel alone or in small groups. At night, they may gather in trees to rest. Roosting together may shelter them from wind and help protect them from predators.

Their antennae and eyes send signals to the brain. The monarchs use this information to determine which direction to fly.

During their long journey, monarchs take rest stops to feed on energy-giving nectar.

FOX SCOUTS

Without clues or knowing what to look for, can you find the **24** objects hidden in this scene?

FUN FACT

Red foxes have more than 20 different calls.

HUNTER'S MOON

In the lonely night silence,
a hunter's moon shines,
bright and round.
Low along the cattails,
a fox creeps.
Its fluffy tail catches a moonbeam.
Wild geese take flight.

LAUGH ATTACK

Why was the fox upset?
Because everyone kept hounding him

**How far can a fox
run into the woods?**
*Halfway. After that, it is
running out of the woods.*

**What did the fox do
for the talent show?**
The foxtrot

How do foxes travel?
Fur-st class

LAUGH ATTACK

**What did the snake say
to his little sister?**
"Stop being such a rattle-tail!"

**What do you call a
flying skunk?**
A smelly-copter

Knock, knock.
Who's there?
Odor.
Odor who?
**Odor skunks are wiser
than younger skunks.**

Knock, knock.
Who's there?
Bat.
Bat who?
I'll bat you can't guess.

**What is black and white
and blue all over?**
A skunk holding its breath

**What is a snake's
favorite state?**
Hississippi

**How many skunks does it
take to change a light bulb?**
A phew

What do bats do for fun?
They hang out with their friends.

**What kind of shoes
do reptiles wear?**
Snakers

What time do ducks wake up?
At the quack of dawn

HELP THE CARTOONISTS!

These cartoons are missing their captions. Write your own punch lines,
then check out the cartoonists' original gags on page 138.

LEAPFROG

Find a path from **START** to **FINISH** by hopping from frog to frog.
The correct path uses frogs that are juggling an even number of objects.

START

BONUS!
Which objects start with the letter P?

BONUS!
Find the two matching frogs.

BONUS!
How many objects are being juggled along the right path? Add 'em up!

FINISH

50

What do frogs do in the winter?

In places that have cold, snowy winters, frogs hibernate. Their heart rate and breathing rate slow down. The frogs stay fairly still and use very little energy until spring.

Frogs that live in water—such as bullfrogs—hibernate underwater, on the bottom of a stream or pond. They may slowly swim around from time to time, but they mainly lie still.

Frogs that live on land—such as wood frogs—hibernate on land, usually in burrows or under the cover of leaves or rocks. Wood frogs hide in small spaces, then parts of their bodies freeze. They have a lot of sugar in their brains, hearts, and other vital organs. The sugar works as an antifreeze and prevents these organs from freezing. Ice forms in other parts of the frog's body, but the frog will thaw out and warm up in the spring, ready to go.

I'm a wood frog.

LAUGH ATTACK

What did the frog order for lunch?

French flies and a large croak

What do frogs like to get in the mail?

Flyers

Where do frogs take notes?

On lily pads

What kind of cars do frogs drive?

Hop rods

Why did the frog go to the hospital?

It needed a hop-eration.

20/20 VISION

Look closely to find all the pairs of numbers next to each other that add up to 20. These pairs may go across, up, down, or diagonally. Every number will be used as part of one pair.

12	17	3	14	7	16	4
1	8	15	6	13	10	3
19	10	10	5	10	17	12
16	2	9	11	19	8	18
4	7	18	6	1	9	2
13	0	20	14	15	5	11

LAUGH ATTACK

What do you call an owl magician?
Whoo-dini

What kind of bird always wears armor?
A knight owl

Why did the owl say "woof"?
She was learning a new language.

Knock, knock.
Who's there?
Owls.
Owls who?
Of course they do.

What subject do owls like to study?
Owl-gebra

MAKE A MATCH

Find three pairs of matching owls.

Why do whitetail deer raise their tails when they run away?

They do this to send a danger signal to other deer. Whitetails travel in groups and look out for enemies together. If one detects a hint of trouble, such as an unfamiliar smell, it will raise its tail halfway up. This shows that the deer is alert. If the deer decides that the danger is real, it will lift its tail straight up like a flag to warn the others. Sometimes, it will also wave the tail back and forth. The deer's raised tail tells the group to run away.

How high can whitetail deer jump?

Adult whitetail deer have been seen leaping over 8-foot-high fences. This ability helps them stay alive. If the animals are being chased by a predator, they need to be able to leap over obstacles in their way. Because of its jumping skills, a deer can easily clear tall fences and large rocks. Deer can jump high thanks to their strong hind legs. The animals' hooves also help. The hooves are tough on the outside with a softer inside. This gives the animals a cushion when they land a big jump.

THE BUCK STOPS HERE

There's a visitor in the woods! Can you find the objects hidden in this scene?

cotton candy

baseball cap

bird

toothbrush

artist's brush

bowl

heart

domino

light bulb

carrot

ice-cream bar

snake

mallet

CALLING ALL BIRD-LEG WORDS!

Use the clues to name words with "bird legs" (double L's) in them.
We did the first one for you.

1. Opposite of good-bye
   H E L L O

2. Opposite of push
   _ _ _ _

3. Ten dimes
   _ _ _ _ _ _

4. Sick
   _ _ _

5. Not sick
   _ _ _ _

6. Make cold
   _ _ _ _ _ _

7. Long passageway between rooms
   _ _ _ _ _

8. Long passageway between buildings
   _ _ _ _ _

9. Two sizes
   _ _ _ _

   _ _ _ _ _ _

BONUS!
What other bird-leg words do you see pictured in the scene?

CANNONBALL!

HELLO, BILL

REALLY?

ALLOW ME.

CALL ME!

THRILLING!

WILL DO.

KIDS' SCIENCE QUESTIONS

How do birds defend their territory?

The sparrows in the photo below may look as if they are playing. Actually, they are fighting over territory.

Each bird needs a place to build a nest, plus habitat for finding food and rearing its young.

Often when animals such as birds and squirrels seem to be playing, they are really trying to chase each other away.

A lot of "talk" that means "Go away!"

One bird tries to chase the other away by diving and swooping at it.

Birds perch in open areas where they can see their territory and where other birds can see them.

LAUGH ATTACK

Where do birds stay when they're on vacation?

At a cheep hotel

Why do birds fly south for the winter?

Because it's too far to walk

What do you call two birds that fall in love?

Tweet-hearts

What kind of birds stick together?

Vel-crows

RACCOON CAMPOUT

Can you find at least **22** differences between these two pictures?

KIDS' SCIENCE QUESTIONS

Do raccoons wash their food before eating it?

No, this is a commonly held myth! Raccoons do sometimes dip foods like fruits and nuts in water but not to wash them off. Instead, they're trying to examine the meal. These critters use their sense of touch to investigate unfamiliar objects. The animals' hands are very sensitive, especially when wet. By dunking their hands in water while holding food, they're able to get a better sense of what they're about to eat.

I'm an omnivore! I eat plants and meat.

Why do raccoon eyes seem to glow?

The eyes seem to glow because light is reflected by a shiny layer at the back of the eye. This shiny layer helps the raccoon see at night. Like a person's eyes, raccoons' eyes have cells that sense light as it goes through them. The raccoon's shiny layer acts like a mirror behind those cells, and it reflects light back through them. That gives the cells a second chance to catch the light.

Are bats really blind?

Bats are not blind, but no animal can see in complete darkness. Since many kinds of bats hunt insects at night, they have an additional trick called echolocation for finding their way in the dark. The bat uses its mouth (some also use their noses!) to create sounds that bounce off nearby objects, such as a moth. When the sound comes back to the bat's ears, the bat can tell where the object is. Using echolocation, the bat can find its prey and snatch it in midair.

LAUGH ATTACK

Knock, knock.
Who's there?
Vampire.
Vampire who?
The Vampire State Building.

What is the only animal at a baseball game?
A bat

What keeps bats going?
Batteries

A NIGHTTIME FLIGHT

Help the bat find its way back to its cave.
Use the letters along the correct path to solve the riddle.

FINISH

START

What is a bat's favorite game?

_ _ _ _ - _ _ _ _ - _ _ _ _ _

PRAIRIE POP-UP

There are **14** prairie dogs hidden in the grids below. Here's how to find them:
Each numbered square tells you how many of the empty squares touching it contain
a prairie dog. The squares with prairie dogs can be above,
below, left, right, or diagonal from the numbered square. Place an **X** on
squares that can't have a prairie dog. Then draw a prairie dog or a circle
on squares that have a prairie dog.

0			2
	4		
			1
2		1	

HINTS:

- Put an X on all the squares touching a zero.

- Look at the sides of the big grid, where large numbers may make it more obvious where prairie dogs are hiding.

- A prairie dog cannot go in a square that has a number.

1		0			
				4	
4		3			
				1	
3		1			
				1	

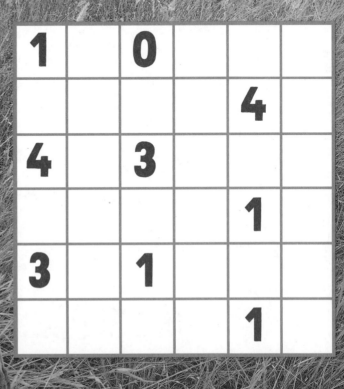

Where do prairie dogs live?

Prairie dogs often live in big "towns" made up of small burrows dug next to one another. Some towns have hundreds of thousands of prairie dogs. The openings look like small craters surrounded by dirt. Prairie dogs usually go only a short way from their burrows to eat grasses and other plants.

Why do prairie dogs have different warning calls?

Prairie dogs use many different sounds to call to one another. They use some of these sounds to warn other prairie dogs when an animal comes hunting for them. Using different calls, they can tell other prairie dogs whether the hunter is a hawk, a coyote, or a snake.

Why would prairie dogs want to tell their enemies apart? One reason is that different alarm calls allow prairie dogs to use the best escape route for each enemy. For a coyote alarm, all the prairie dogs run to their burrow entrances. They watch the coyote so it can't sneak up on them. When a hawk alarm sounds, all the prairie dogs in the hawk's path dive into their burrows. (Hawks are speedier than coyotes, and the prairie dogs don't want to take any chances.) After hearing a human alarm, prairie dogs run to their burrows and almost all of them go underground. Hearing the different calls tells prairie dogs how to react so they have the best chance of survival.

TEAM SPIRIT!

Let's go, team! Can you find the open book, fishhook, ruler, toothbrush, needle, parrot, flashlight, banana, pencil, cup and straw, crescent moon, golf club, wishbone, spoon, fork, tube of toothpaste, comb, teacup, crown, saltshaker, and fish hidden in this scene?

What's an alligator's favorite card game?
. . . .
sueg

Where do alligators go on vacation?
. . . .
Wherever the GPS navi-gator takes them

LATER, 'GATOR

This alligator wants to soak up some sun.
Help him reach his favorite spot by finding a path from **START** to **FINISH**.

KIDS' SCIENCE QUESTIONS

Why do alligators have black bumps on their faces?

Little black bumps cover an alligator's jaws. The bumps are sensors. Humans and other animals have many kinds of sensors, such as those in the tongue for tasting and those in the skin for feeling. When a sensor is activated, nerves send information from the sensor to the brain. For instance, when you eat chocolate, sensors in your tongue tell your brain you're tasting something sweet. The sensors on the alligator's jaws help it find food. They detect ripples in the water made by another animal. The sensors send a signal to the brain, alerting it that something is nearby. Then the alligator knows to snap up the meal.

PIGEON PAIRS

Each pigeon has an exact match. Can you find all **12** pairs of pigeons?

What is a pigeon's favorite drink?

Hot coo-coo

Why are
pigeons so good
at baseball?
. . . .
Because they
always know how
to get home

TURTLE CROSSING

This puzzle is crawling with **27** kinds of turtles. Their names fit into the grid in just one way. Use the number of letters in each word as a clue to where it might fit. No hurry. Take your time.

XING

Word List

3 Letters
BOG
BOX
MAP

4 Letters
MUSK
WOOD

5 Letters
BLACK
GREEN

7 Letters
PAINTED
SPOTTED

8 Letters
FALSE MAP
FLATBACK
SNAPPING
STINKPOT
TERRAPIN

9 Letters
BLANDING'S
HAWKSBILL
YELLOW MUD

10 Letters
EASTERN MUD
LOGGERHEAD
POND SLIDER

11 Letters
KEMP'S RIDLEY
LEATHERBACK
OLIVE RIDLEY
RIVER COOTER

14 Letters
RED-EARED SLIDER
SPINY SOFTSHELL

15 Letters
SMOOTH
 SOFTSHELL

SLOW

LOGGERHEAD

BUNNY TREE HOUSE

These bunnies are having lots of fun! Can you find the objects hidden in this scene?

BONUS!

Can you find the candle, needle, knit hat, fishhook, and golf club?

shoe

bell

crown

heart

baseball bat

crescent moon

mug

wishbone

pencil

bat

spoon

LAUGH ATTACK

What is a rabbit's favorite candy?
Lolli-hops

Where do bunnies live?
In a rabbitat

Emma: How do you catch a unique rabbit?
Luke: How?
Emma: Unique up on it! How do you catch a tame rabbit?
Luke: I don't know.
Emma: The tame way

If you find a rabbit eating your dictionary, what should you do?
Take the words right out of its mouth.

Where do rabbits go when they want to hear singing?
To the hop-era

Why don't rabbits get hot in the summer?
They have hare-conditioning.

What do you get when you cross a rabbit with a spiderweb?
A hare net

What do you call a rabbit that works on cars?
A jackrabbit

What do you call a rabbit that is angry in the summer?
A hot cross bunny

Why did the dust bunny use the computer?
To go on the linternet

What do you call a line of rabbits walking backward?
A receding hare line

CHECK . . . AND DOUBLE CHECK

Can you find at least **11** differences between these two pictures?

WHAT'S WRONG?

Which things in this picture are silly? It's up to you!

What do beavers eat for breakfast?

Oatmeal

BUMPER ★ CARS

OVERSLEPT

Bernard didn't hear his alarm go off and "bearly" woke up in time for spring!
Can you find the objects hidden in this scene?

Why do bears sleep all winter?

Because no one's brave enough to wake them up

BONUS!
Can you find
the kite, sailboat,
and needle?

egg

shoe

fish

spoon

teacup

crown

hat

pair of pants

How do bears survive winter?

During winter, foods that bears eat, like berries and salmon, become scarce. To survive this food shortage, bears hibernate through the winter months. They prepare for hibernation by eating a lot in late summer. Some species will eat about 90 pounds of food a day! They store the fats and nutrients from these meals in their bodies.

As winter approaches, the bears enter their dens and begin hibernating.

They live off the nutrients and fats they collected. To save energy, their heartrates drop and their breathing slows. Some hibernating bears breathe only about once a minute. But unlike other hibernating animals, a bear's body temperature doesn't fall very low. This allows it to react more quickly if it senses danger near its den. Because of this, many scientists call bears "super hibernators." Bears typically hibernate for several months. Then they emerge from their dens ready for some yummy snacks.

Why do bears sometimes stand up on their hind legs?

Some people think bears stand on their hind legs when angry or threatened. But that's often not true. Bears usually stand up when they want a better view of their surroundings. They may also get on their hind legs if they smell something unfamiliar and want to sniff the air. Certain species of bears become very tall when standing upright. Adult brown bears can rise seven feet high. And Kodiak bears, a species found only in Alaska, can measure ten feet tall when standing!

I'm a brown bear.

A LEAP OF LOGIC

It's time for the annual Lakeside County frog-jumping contest. Taylor and two of her friends have entered their frogs. Using the clues below, can you figure out whose frog is whose and what place each frog took in the contest?

Use the chart to keep track of your answers. Put an **X** in each box that can't be true and an **O** in boxes that match.

	Freddie	Spot	Hoppy	1st	2nd	3rd
Taylor						
Madison						
Cameron						

1. Taylor's frog finished after Hoppy.
2. Madison's frog finished before Cameron's frog and Spot.
3. Freddie finished second.

What does a frog sit on?
A toadstool

What's a frog's favorite flower?
A croakus

What is the greenest side of a frog?
The outside

What does a frog that likes barbecue say?
"Rib-it. Rib it."

What happened to the frog that parked illegally?
He got toad.

What do you call a toad that eats all the flies?
A frog hog

KIDS' SCIENCE QUESTIONS

What's the difference between a toad and a frog?

A toad is a type of frog. Toads are different from other frogs. Frogs usually live in or around water. Toads, however, dwell in drier spots. Toads also have shorter legs, and they move around by crawling. Other frogs' legs are longer, and they get around by leaping. Perhaps the biggest difference has to do with the animals' skin. Most frogs have moist skin. But toad skin is dry and bumpy.

FROG

TOAD

LIZARD LOOK-ALIKES

Each lizard in the scene has an exact match. Can you find all **10** matching pairs?

FUN FACT

Some lizards can detach their tails when threatened by predators.

What do you get when you cross kangaroos with geckos?

Leaping lizards!

79

A HUM OF ACTIVITY

Can you keep up with a hummingbird? They're the smallest and quickest birds on the planet. Check out these hummingbird facts, then find the **13** objects hidden in this scene.

Your heart beats about 70 to 115 times per minute. During daytime, a hummingbird's heart beats 500 to 1,260 times per minute. Its heart slows down at night to about 50 to 180 beats per minute.

There are more than 320 kinds of humming-birds, and all of them live in North or South America.

Hummingbirds consume about 1.5 times their body weight every day.

Most hummingbirds make a scratchy, squeaky song. But their wings can make a humming sound, which is how they communicate with other hummingbirds.

Hummingbirds eat by sticking their long, skinny bills inside flowers. Then they lap up bugs or the flower's nectar with their long tongues.

Hummingbirds can fly 30 miles per hour.

Hummingbirds are tiny. The largest species is called the giant humming-bird, but it's still only eight inches long.

The bee hummingbird is the smallest bird in the world. It's only about two inches long and weighs as little as two paper clips.

Hummingbirds can fly forward, up, down, and sideways. They're also the only birds that can fly backward and upside down!

UNDERGROUND MAZE

Help Groundhog Greg find his way aboveground
by finding a path from **START** to **FINISH**.

START

FINISH

What is a
groundhog's
favorite color?

Ma-hog-any

Try to say these

TONGUE TWISTERS

three times, fast.

**The groggy groundhog
gargled.**

**The groundhog grabbed a
green gift.**

**Groundhog Greg grew
great grapes.**

**The shy, sleepy groundhog
was shocked to see
his shadow.**

What type of animal is a groundhog?

"Groundhog" is a misleading name. This animal isn't a hog. Instead, it's a type of rodent. Groundhogs belong to the same family as squirrels, chipmunks, and prairie dogs. In fact, groundhogs are one of the largest members of this family, capable of weighing up to 15 pounds.

FUN FACT

Groundhogs are also called "whistle-pigs." They make a whistle-like sound to warn other groundhogs of danger.

Where do groundhogs make their homes?

These quiet mammals are usually found in areas with open meadows and a mix of trees. They spend most of their time underground in burrows. The burrows have different chambers. And these chambers serve different purposes. Some are for sleeping. Others are used as nurseries, where babies are placed. The burrows can be quite long. Some stretch for 66 feet!

What did the cat say to the butterfly?
"You butterfly away."

Why did the kid throw the butter out the window?
To see the butterfly

Knock, knock.
Who's there?
Usher.
Usher who?
Usher do love butterflies.

Why couldn't the butterfly go to the dance?
Because it was a moth ball

What is a butterfly's favorite subject?
Moth-ematics

Knock, knock.
Who's there?
Moth.
Moth who?
I moth tell you that I like you.

What does a chatty caterpillar become?
A social butterfly.

How do caterpillars swim laps?
They do the butterfly

Where do butterflies sleep?
On cater-pillows

What are caterpillars afraid of?
Dog-erpillars

TIC TAC ROW

Each of these butterflies has something in common with the other two butterflies in the same row—across, down, and diagonally. For example, in the top row across, each butterfly is orange. Can you tell what's alike in each row?

Try to say these

TONGUE TWISTERS

three times, fast.

A creeping caterpillar crawls by the creek.

Betty Butterfly bought better butter.

HIDE-AND-SEEK

These foxes found some good hiding places!
Can you find the objects hidden in this scene?

glove

teapot

baseball bat

boot

closed umbrella

pencil

broccoli

football

fried egg

car

saw

artist's brush

fish

comb

ladder

key

KIDS' SCIENCE QUESTIONS

How do fox pups learn survival skills?

Fox pups, also known as kits, are born in the spring. After about a month, they are old enough to go outside. Then pup siblings often play around with one another near the opening to the den. Playtime helps the foxes learn survival skills. For instance, the pups wrestle each other, which helps them practice their hunting skills. They also practice catching prey brought home by their parents.
Once fall arrives, the pups are ready to set off on their own.

> We'll stay with our parents for about 7 months.

Why is a red fox's hearing so good?

Red foxes have flexible, large, pointy ears. They can twist their ears almost all the way around toward the noises they hear. This can help them figure out exactly where a sound is coming from. Red foxes can hear sounds we can't, including higher pitches. In fact, a red fox's hearing is so sharp, it can detect rodents digging underground!

DON'T BUG ME

These **18** bug words can wiggle their way into this puzzle. Their names fit into the grid in just one way. Use the number of letters in each word as a clue to where it might fit. Once you fill them in, unscramble the highlighted letters to find the answer to the riddle.

3 Letters	5 Letters	7 Letters	9 Letters
ANT	ROACH	LADYBUG	BUTTERFLY
FLY	**6 Letters**	TERMITE	DRAGONFLY
4 Letters	BEETLE	**8 Letters**	**11 Letters**
FLEA	CICADA	HONEYBEE	GRASSHOPPER
GNAT	LOCUST	KATYDIDS	**13 Letters**
MOTH			PRAYING MANTIS
WASP			

Which sport do insects like better than baseball?

— — — — — — — —

RIDDLE SUDOKU

Fill in the squares so that the six letters appear only once in each row, column, and 2 x 3 box. Then read the blue squares to find out the answer to the riddle.

Our Sudoku puzzles use letters instead of numbers.

Riddle:

Where do insects go on vacation?

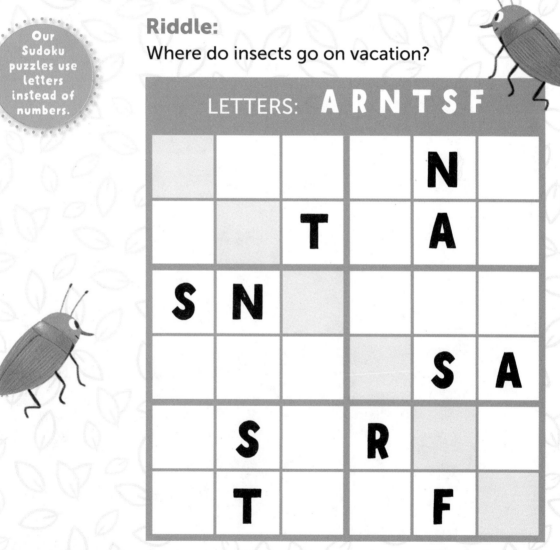

LETTERS: **A R N T S F**

				N	
		T		A	
S	N				
				S	A
	S		R		
	T			F	

Answer:

__ __ __ __ __ __ __

TIC TAC ROW

Each of these birds has something in common with the other two birds in the same row—across, down, and diagonally. For example, in the top row across, each bird is holding a worm. Can you tell what's alike in each row?

Try to say these

TONGUE TWISTERS

three times, fast.

Sparrows sing special silly songs.

Eight eagles equal eight.

How does a scrub jay remember where it placed food?

The scrub jay has a good memory. This is important because a scrub jay needs to remember where to find its food in winter. The scrub jay spends a lot of time storing food in the fall. The bird collects seeds and nuts, then stashes them in little holes in the ground. How does a scrub jay find these hidden foods again? The jay can line itself up with trees, rocks, and other landmarks, then get back to exactly the same spot where it hid a seed or nut—even months after it stored the food.

LAUGH ATTACK

How do baby birds learn to fly?

They just wing it.

What is a bird's favorite food?

A-sparrow-gus

What bird can lift the heaviest weight?

A crane

What are smarter than talking birds?

Spelling bees

What do birds eat for dessert?

Chocolate-chirp cookies

BOOKS NEVER WRITTEN

Check out the titles of these **10** funny books.
See how many you can match with the author.
(**HINT**: Try reading the authors' names out loud!)

_J_ **1.** *How to Catch Worms*

___ **2.** *Speckled Fellows*

___ **3.** *I Look Like an Elk*

___ **4.** *How to Pet an Alligator*

___ **5.** *Spider by Your Foot*

___ **6.** *How Small Are Baby Turtles?*

___ **7.** *Before the Cocoon*

___ **8.** *Frog Chairs*

___ **9.** *What Bears Do Best*

___**10.** *Bug Sandwiches*

A. Justine E.

B. Liz Ardchow

C. Kat R. Pillar

D. Carrie Bou

E. Lily Padd

F. B. Careful

G. Lady Buggs

H. Clem Trees

I. Don Scream

J. Earl E. Bird

SCRAMBLED WORDS

We've jumbled the names of **10** backyard animals. Can you unscramble each set of letters and find the words? Once you have them all, read down the column of boxes to learn the answer to the riddle:

Where do backyard animals keep their food?

AILROLATG   _ _ _ _ [ ] _ _ _ _

NSKAE   _ _ [ ] _ _ _

RAILDZ   _ _ _ [ ] _ _

HSPSARPEROG   _ _ _ _ _ _ [ ] _ _ _ _

EARB   _ _ [ ] _

CONAROC   _ _ _ _ [ ] _ _

BTUTEYRFL   _ _ [ ] _ _ _ _ _ _

TLURTE   _ _ _ [ ] _ _

QUESRRLI   _ _ _ _ _ [ ] _ _

LEK   [ ] _ _

LAUGH ATTACK

Knock, knock.
Who's there?
Baby owl.
Baby owl who?
Baby owl see you later or baby owl just call you.

What is an owl's favorite dessert?
Mice cream

Ally: I know someone who thinks he's an owl.
Owen: Who?
Ally: Now I know two.

Why was the owl a great investigative reporter?
He was always asking, "Who? Who? Who?"

What bird is at every meal?
A swallow

KIDS' SCIENCE QUESTIONS

What does a screech owl sound like?

Screech owls can be hard to spot, even though they often live near wooded suburbs and in parks. These birds blend in well with the trees on which they perch. During the day, screech owls are quiet, which makes them even harder to notice. But it's not unusual to hear their calls at night. One call sounds like the high-pitched whinny of a horse. Another is a bouncing trill, like a rapidly repeating woo or coo.

WHOOO KNOWS?

Night school is a great place to learn! Can you find the objects hidden in this scene?

WHO
WHOM

What is an owl's favorite kind of pepper?

Owl-apeño

chess piece

ring

mitten

fish

trowel

wedge of orange

domino

arrow

sailboat

comb

BONUS!

Can you find the fishhook, safety pin, screwdriver, necklace, crescent moon, drumstick, and hockey stick?

BREAKFAST TIME!

Can you help the bear catch the fish? Use the clues to fill in the blanks. Each word is only one letter different than the one above it.

B E A R

1. What you do to a drum ○ ○ ○ ○

2. Good, better, _____ ○ ○ ○ ○

3. A girl's name, rhymes with jess ○ ○ ○ ○

4. An untidy area ○ ○ ○ ○

5. To fail to hit the ball ○ ○ ○ ○

6. Fog ○ ○ ○ ○

7. Your hand can form this ○ ○ ○ ○

F I S H

LAUGH ATTACK

Why wouldn't the grizzly walk on a gravel road?

It had bear feet.

Why did the bear put his saxophone in the freezer?

To make cool music

SWEET VICTORY

Mary, Barry, and Jerry held a contest to see who could eat the most honey. Can you use the clues to find out which bear ate out of which jar and how each bear placed in the contest?

	PURPLE JAR	GREEN JAR	YELLOW JAR	1st PLACE	2nd PLACE	3rd PLACE
MARY						
BARRY						
JERRY						

Use the chart to keep track of your answers.
Put an **X** in each box that can't be true and an **O** in boxes that match.

1. Jerry and Mary ate more honey than Barry.
2. The bear in second place ate out of the yellow jar.
3. Mary did not eat out of the purple or yellow jar.

Try to say these

TONGUE TWISTERS

three times, fast.

Grumpy grizzlies growl gruffly.

A big black bug bit a big black bear.

BAKING TIME!

There are **8** objects hidden in the scene on the next page. Write each set of colored letters on the same-colored lines to figure out the hidden objects, then find them in the scene!

B B Y R P W S U C A A T I E H L T U L
R N N E O L C N E O N N G K N Y L

_____   _____

_____   _____

_____   _____

_____   _____

KIDS' SCIENCE QUESTIONS

Do mice really like cheese?

A lot of cartoon mice seem to love cheese, but there's no reason to think that real mice would like it. Mice survive by eating seeds and other plant materials. They probably could not digest cheese very well. Scientists at Manchester Metropolitan University in England did experiments to see which foods were the favorites of several kinds of animals. When mice had a choice, they didn't pick cheese. They chose chocolate and other foods that have a lot of sugar. Eating a lot of sugar would not be healthy for us, or even for mice. But sugar is food energy and hard to find outside of a kitchen or grocery store. In the wild, most mice can eat all the sugar they can find and burn it all just in their daily activities.

BIRD SUDOKU

Draw or write each bird's name in the squares so that the six kinds
of birds appear only once in each row, column, and 2 x 3 box.

LAUGH ATTACK

**What has eight legs
and walks on webs?**

Four ducks

**What does a chickadee say
when it's very hungry?**

"Long time, no seed."

LAUGH ATTACK

What is the saddest bird?
The blue jay

Knock, knock.
Who's there?
Wren.
Wren who?
Wren you're finished, please put it away.

What do you call someone who treats sick ducks?
A duck-tor

What do you call a hawk that can draw and play the guitar?
Talon-ted

Knock, knock.
Who's there?
Allison.
Allison who?
Allison to the birds every morning.

What do ducks eat for breakfast?
Milk and quackers

What did the duck say when its meal arrived?
"Put it on my bill."

Why should you always have ducks on your basketball team?
They always make fowl shots.

What do you get when you cross a ghost and a bird?
The grim cheeper

Why are geese poor drivers?
Because all they do is honk

"Your first migration, I presume?"

THE GRUMPY SKUNK

The grumpy skunk was in a funk.
He held his nose because he stunk.
Thought it might help to splash and dunk.
He jumped into a pond, *kerplunk*.
When he climbed out, the skunk had shrunk!

Now grumpy skunk is small and dinky,
Half as big and rather slinky,
Half the fur both white and inky
Right down to his little pinkie.
But at least he's half as stinky.

SMELL STOPPER

To find the answer to the riddle below, first cross out all the pairs of matching letters. Then write the remaining letters in order in the spaces beneath the riddle.

TT	YO	XX	EE	RR	HH	PP
AA	MM	QQ	JJ	FF	UH	XX
OL	BB	NN	GG	II	CC	YY
DD	VV	KK	LL	WW	DI	OO
UU	RR	TS	FF	ZZ	AA	JJ
CC	XX	EE	MM	II	PP	NO
QQ	NN	VV	SE	KK	FF	LL

How do you stop a skunk from smelling?

__ __ __ __ __ __ __

__ __ __ __ __ __ __ __ .

Try to say this

TONGUE TWISTER

three times, fast.

A skunk sat on a stump, and the stump said the skunk stunk, and the skunk said the stump stunk.

FALL FUN

Compare these two pictures. Can you find at least **13** differences?

TONGUE TWISTERS

Ollie Owl always wears only orange overalls.

Itchy inchworms itch worse after itching.

KNOT AGAIN!

This snake's all twisted up! Can you find the objects hidden in this scene?

BONUS!
Can you find the crescent moon, spoon, and horn?

paper clip

duck

crown

camel

gingerbread man

egg

star

banana

bowl

bell

LAUGH ATTACK

Why do you measure a snake in inches?

Because snakes don't have feet

What snakes are good at doing sums?

Adders

What do snakes use to cut paper?

Scissssors

What kind of snake keeps its car the cleanest?

A windshield viper

Why did the snake go to the toy store?

To get a new rattle

KIDS' SCIENCE QUESTIONS

How do snakes climb trees?

Not all snakes are able to climb trees, but some are surprisingly good at it. To climb a tree, a snake makes the scales on its underside stick out and catch on the rough parts of the bark. Parts of the bark may stick out far enough to support the snake's weight. Then the snake can push against these parts to slither up the tree.

The snake may also curve into an S shape and push the sides of its body outward, against the inner edges of a groove in the bark. It can cling to the tree with the front of its body, then pull up its lower body to get another grip and keep climbing. Then it can extend the front of its body higher for another

grip. By switching back and forth between these two grips, the snake can climb the tree.

But this method is not perfect. Snakes often fall out of the trees they are climbing.

Why can't you fool a snake?

You can't pull its leg

107

To find the answer to the riddle below, first cross out all the pairs of matching letters.
Then write the remaining letters in order in the spaces beneath the riddle.

MM	BB	CC	KK	IT	ZZ	HH
QQ	NN	GE	SS	JJ	WW	II
TS	AA	RR	VV	LL	DD	FF
YY	OO	XX	AB	EE	PP	BB
GG	UZ	CC	AA	HH	NN	ZZ
WW	MM	LL	TT	DD	ZC	KK
UT	QQ	EE	JJ	SS	II	RR

What kind of haircut does a bee get?

— — — — — — —

— — — — — — — —.

STICKY STUMPER

Help the honey bee find its way through the honeycomb from **START** to **FINISH**.
Use the letters along the correct path to answer the riddle.

What would bears be without bees?

— — — —

Try to say these

TONGUE TWISTERS

three times, fast.

Big Billy Bee buzzes by Benny Beetle.

Busy bees bumble by.

BIRDS OF A FEATHER

Each bird on the top wire has a twin below with the same coloring.
Can you find each twin?

BONUS!

What do the birds on each wire have in common?

For example, the birds on the top wire all have their tails down.

1

2

3

4

110

Why do female birds choose the brightest-colored males as mates?

Usually, the colorful birds we see are males. Female birds are attracted to their bright colors and prefer to mate with the most colorful males they can find. Why is this so? In many species, male and female birds work together to raise the young. Each female wants to choose the healthiest male to help her. Feathers can often tell a female bird a lot about a male's well-being. Bright feathers contain a special pigment, or substance that gives color. Healthy males have an easier time producing this pigment, and they grow brighter feathers. Sick birds have a harder time producing the pigment, and their feathers are duller. So, by choosing the brightest males, females get the healthiest mates.

LAUGH ATTACK

Knock, knock.
Who's there?
Cook.
Cook who?
Nice bird impression! Now will you let me in?

What do sick birds need?
Tweet-ment

What bird can lift the heaviest weight?
A crane

What do you call a bird that smells bad?
A foul fowl

Who leads the bird band?
The con-duck-tor

WHAT'S WRONG?

Which things in this picture are silly? It's up to you!

What did
one wolf say
to another?

· · · · · · · · · · · · · · ·

"How's it going?"

AAROO!

Do wolves really howl at the moon?

No, this is a myth. Howling may be heard at night, but wolves aren't calling out to the moon. Instead, wolves howl to communicate. A howling wolf may be trying to bring pack members together, or it may make this noise to protect territory. Howling works best over long distances. A howl can travel six miles in a forest and ten miles in an area without trees.

How big are gray wolf packs?

Gray-wolf packs usually have around five to eight members, but some include more than thirty wolves. A pack is made of two adult leaders (called the alpha male and female) and their offspring. Pack members travel and hunt together. They also care for each other. Wolves have been seen bringing food to injured members of their pack!

Our pack's range can be between 80 and 300 miles.

DEER DASH

The race is on for these deer. Without clues or knowing what to look for, can you find the **16** objects hidden in the scene? Ready, set, go!

PLACE 35.01

1ST

2ND

35.01

LAUGH ATTACK

Knock, knock.
Who's there?
Deer.
Deer who?
Deer to be different.

What do deer have that no other animals have?
Baby deer

Which friends did the baby deer invite to her birthday party?
Her nearest and deer-est friends

What do you call a baby deer that is eating grass?
A fawn mower

A duck, a deer, and a skunk went out to dinner. When the waiter came with the check, the deer said he didn't have a buck, and the skunk said he didn't have a scent. So they put it on the duck's bill!

What is a female deer's favorite ice cream flavor?
Cookie doe

Which deer have the shortest legs?
The smallest ones

What deer costs a dollar?
A buck

My parents loved to eat pretzels.

SCALY STUMPER

Draw the missing reptiles in the blank spaces so each reptile appears only once in each row and column.

LAUGH ATTACK

Where do lizards go to get their tails put back on?
A re-tail store

What do lizards like to eat with their hamburgers?
French flies

What kind of snake likes dessert?
A pie-thon

How do turtles call each other?
With their shell phone!

REPTILE REPORT

Some of these reptile facts are true and some are false.
Can you tell which are true?

1. All reptiles are cold-blooded.
T OR F

2. All reptiles lay eggs.
T OR F

3. The Komodo dragon is the smallest species of lizard.
T OR F

4. Snakes are able to smell with their tongues.
T OR F

5. Reptiles can breathe through their skin.
T OR F

6. There are more than 8,000 species of reptiles.
T OR F

7. Some snakes can go months without eating.
T OR F

8. A turtle can lay only one egg at a time.
T OR F

9. All reptiles have scales.
T OR F

10. Turtles don't have feeling in their shells.
T OR F

PARTY PATH

Calvin has arrived at the location of his cousin's birthday party, but where is everyone? Help him get to the party by starting at the **9** in the top corner. You may move to a new box by adding **4** or subtracting **5**. Move up, down, left, or right.

START

9	15	18	10	15	19
4	7	11	21	16	20
8	12	15	5	12	15
15	11	10	14	17	10
12	17	6	9	13	14
9	18	21	7	20	18

FINISH

What did the rabbit get for her birthday?
. . . .
A 14-carrot ring

118

SALAD WORKS

Can you find at least **18** differences between these two pictures?

THE MOOSE IS LOOSE

We let an artist loose on this moose. Read some moose facts, then find the **13** objects hidden in this scene.

Moose can't see very well, but their hearing and sense of smell are excellent.

Male moose grow antlers every spring and lose them in January.

Moose antlers can grow 6 feet across, and weigh up to 85 pounds.

A full-grown moose can weigh as much as 1,500 pounds.

The average life span of a moose is 15 to 20 years.

Moose have no front teeth on the top. They grab plants with their lips and chew with their back teeth.

Moose are a type of deer.

Moose eat grass, shrubs, moss, and pinecones.

A baby moose can run faster than a person by the time it's just 5 days old. Adult moose can run up to 35 miles an hour.

Why does a moose have a flap of skin under its chin?

These flaps of skin are called dewlaps or bells. Both males and females have them. Scientists don't know exactly what they are for, but they have some ideas. Some scientists think it's possible the flaps are used to attract mates. The flaps might also be used to show dominance.

Can moose swim?

Yes, they can! Moose are actually quite good at swimming. They can swim six miles an hour for two hours at a time. The animals have nostril flaps they can close to keep water out of their noses. What's more, moose are covered in hollow hair, which traps air. This helps a moose to stay afloat in water. Moose go swimming in summer to cool off and to search for aquatic plants to eat.

BEETLE MATCHUP

Each beetle in the scene has an exact match.
Can you find all the matching pairs?

FUN FACT

Beetles can be found almost everywhere in the world, except polar regions and the ocean.

Why do insects hate the rain?

A lot of insects disappear when rain begins to fall. It's interesting to think about what they may feel, even though scientists don't think the simple brains of insects can have feelings like ours. To think about why insects avoid rain, imagine what it would be like to be an insect. How hard would it be to walk as water rushed across the ground? How hard would it be to fly as gobs of water splashed down? Also, the body of an insect can't generate much heat. Insects depend on heat from the sun and air to keep their bodies warm enough to work. Since rainwater is cold, it makes sense that insects would avoid it.

LAUGH ATTACK

Knock, knock.
Who's there?
Bug spray.
Bug spray who?
Bug spray that birds and snakes will stay away.

What did Papa Lightning Bug say to Mama Lightning Bug?
"Isn't Junior bright?"

What kind of bug tells time?
A clock-roach

What do you call a bug that can jump over a cup?
A glasshopper

How do bugs talk?
They use bee-mail.

NEST QUEST

There are **14** eggs hidden safely in these nests. Here's how to find them: Each numbered square tells you how many of the empty squares touching it contain an egg. The squares with eggs can be above, below, left, right, or diagonal from the numbered square. Place an **X** on squares that can't have an egg. Then draw an egg on squares that have an egg.

HINTS:

- An egg cannot go in a square that has a number.

- In both grids, start by putting an X in all four of the squares touching the zero square. That will give you three squares to put in eggs that are around the square numbered 3.

- Remember that eggs can go only in squares that touch a numbered square.

Grid 1 (4×4):

	1	0	
3		2	
	2		1

Grid 2 (6×6):

		1			1
4					
		2			2
4		3			
		2		3	
2				0	

CATCHING BREAKFAST

Can you help the early bird catch the worm? Use the clues to fill in the blanks.
Each word is only one letter different than the one above it.

B I R D

1. To tie up

2. A musical group

3. A magician's stick

4. To wish for something

5. A toad's skin might have one

6. Not hot, but not cold

W O R M

FUN FACT

Robins can eat up to 14 feet worth of earthworms a day.

Try to say these

TONGUE TWISTERS

three times, fast.

Squirming swans squabble with squawking quails.

Flocks flee fallen trees.

A gaggle of giddy geese.

Pheasants present plenty of pleasant presents.

Why do spring peepers make so much noise in spring?

The spring peeper is a loud little frog. Its tiny body makes a big bell-like sound. The sound of many peepers calling at once is an early sign of spring. Peepers are quiet most of the year. In the spring, the frogs mate and lay their eggs. That's when males call to attract females. By grouping together, males make a racket that brings in females from all around. After a month or so, the mating season ends, and the frogs become quiet once again.

You can identify us by the dark X-shaped mark on our backs.

Why is a frog's skin slimy?

The reason for a frog's slimy skin has to do with the way it breathes. Frogs are able to breathe through their skin. They can do this because their skin absorbs a gas from the air called oxygen. This is the same gas humans take in when we inhale through our mouths and noses. Almost all living things, including frogs and humans, need the gas to survive. But a frog's skin must be moist to absorb this gas. So, frogs produce a sticky mucus that covers their bodies to keep them breathing.

FROG SUDOKU

Draw or write each frog's color in the squares so that the six kinds
of frogs appear only once in each row, column, and 2 x 3 box.

Try to say these

TONGUE TWISTERS

three times, fast.

Five fun-loving frogs.

Four fat frogs flying past fast.

ALL-NIGHT DINER

Animals come from all over to hang out at this diner.
Can you find the objects hidden in this scene?

fishhook

cane

pennant

glove

baseball bat

envelope

sock

paintbrush

crescent moon

whale

balloon

crayon

closed umbrella

plunger

TONGUE TWISTER

Brown bears baked braided bread.

HOOTIE'S all-night diner

DRAW A CARTOON BEAR

Follow these steps to draw a bear on the next page.
Or use your imagination to draw your own bear.

1. Start with a circle for the skull. Draw a large oval behind it for the jaw. Add the nose.

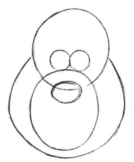

2. Define the snout by drawing a circle around the nose. Add eyes.

3. Draw a downturned mouth and slanting eyebrows. Don't forget ears!

4. Flatten the top of the head a little bit. Finish up with a furry coat and other details. Ta-da!

What do you call a bear with no fur?
. . . .
A bare bear

What do you call a bear standing in the rain?
. . . .
A drizzly bear

TONGUE TWISTER

Betty brought both bears.

TONGUE TWISTER

Brown bears barely notice noisy neighbors.

FIRST FLIGHT

These eagles are ready to leave the nest.
Can you find the objects hidden in this scene?

What does
an eagle use
to write?
·················
A bald-point pen.

sailboat

drumstick

fish

crown

mitten

comb

wishbone

candle

What are the largest eagles that ever lived in the history of planet Earth?

The largest eagle ever was the Haast's eagle of what is now New Zealand. The bird had a wingspan of 6½ to 10 feet and weighed 22 to 33 pounds. After humans arrived in the 1300s, they began to kill off the eagle's main food, a flightless bird called the moa, and the Haast's eagle was extinct by the 1700s.

Fossils show that an even larger bird of prey lived more than 7 million years ago in what is now South America. *Argentavis magnificens* was actually more like a vulture than an eagle. It had a wingspan of 19½ to 26 feet and weighed about 175 pounds.

Argentavis

Haast's eagle

The bony ridge shades the ey from sunlight.

Eagles look stern because of the bony ridge (covered with skin and feathers) above each eye.

An inner (third) eyelid is somewhat transparent. The eagle sees through it when it blinks!

Compared with human eyes, an eagle's eye has far more special cells that make distant images sharp.

The lore area, between the eye and nostril, has short feathers, giving the eye a clear line of sight.

133

THE LAST LAUGH

What kind of sandwiches do bears like?
Growled cheese sandwiches

Knock, knock.
Who's there?
Wolf pack.
Wolf pack who?
Wolf pack some food and go on a picnic.

What do you get when you cross a turtle with a porcupine?
A slowpoke

What did the moose say as she was playing the piano?
"That's moosic to my ears."

Porcupine #1: What do you think of my coat?
Porcupine #2: Looking sharp!

What do you call a lost wolf?
A where-wolf

What did the duck wear to the ball?
A ducks-edo

What did the fox say when she saw her friend for the first time in a long time?
"You're a sight fur sore eyes!"

Knock, knock.
Who's there?
Thea.
Thea who?
Thea later, alligator.

What is a mouse's favorite game?
Hide-and-squeak

ANSWERS

Page 2

Page 3

Page 4

Page 7

Pages 8–9

Page 10

Pages 14–15

Page 16

ANSWERS

Pages 18–19

1. P
2. O
3. U
4. E
5. A
6. R
7. P
8. M
9. J

What do you get if you mix a rabbit and a snake?

A JUMP ROPE

Page 21

Page 22

1. The sports seasons are getting longer. I can't find any time to hibernate.
2. My name is also Teddy!
3. May I stay up one more month, Mom?
4. If you don't start flossing regularly, you're going to end up a gummy bear.

Page 23

Page 24

Page 26

Page 28

LETTERS: A C E H S W

C	W	E	S	A	H
S	A	H	E	W	C
H	E	S	W	C	A
W	C	A	H	S	E
A	H	W	C	E	S
E	S	C	A	H	W

CASHEW

Pages 30–31

Page 32

red eyes stripes tongue out	stripes orange feet	stripes blue on a leaf
hopping tongue out	red eyes hopping blue orange feet	hopping on a leaf
tongue out dots blue	dots orange feet	red eyes dots on a leaf

ANSWERS

Page 33

What do you say to a frog who needs a ride?
"HOP IN!"

Page 34

Why don't rabbits get hot in the summertime?
THEY HAVE HARE-CONDITIONING.

How does a grizzly bear stop a movie?

It presses the "paws" button.

Pages 36–37

Page 38

Page 40

DOVE   PIGEON
CROW   PARROT
HAWK   SPARROW
SWAN   PENGUIN
ROBIN   FLAMINGO
STORK   CARDINAL
GOOSE

Why do hummingbirds hum?
BECAUSE THEY DON'T KNOW THE WORDS

Page 44

Page 46

ANSWERS

Page 49

1. I need a new scent.
2. Why do I have to get up so early? I hate worms.
3. I'll never understand how humans do that.
4. You'll never guess what I had for dinner.

Page 50

Page 52

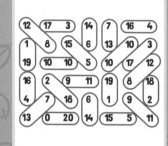

Page 53

Page 55

Page 56

1. Hello
2. Pull
3. Dollar
4. Ill
5. Well
6. Chill
7. Hall
8. Alley
9. Tall, Small

BONUS:
Here are a few. Perhaps you found others. Ball, ballerina, balloons, grill, Jell-O, pillow, shell, umbrella, wall, well.

Page 58

Page 61

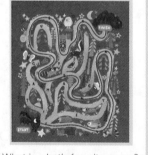

What is a bat's favorite game?
FLY-AND-SEEK

Page 62

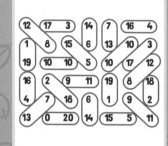

ANSWERS

Page 64

Page 65

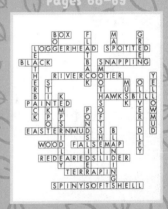

What did the elk say to its loud roommate?

· · · · · · · · · · · · · · · · ·

"Moose you be so noisy?"

Pages 66–67

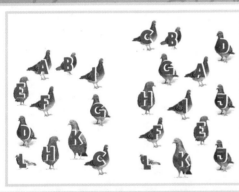

Pages 68–69

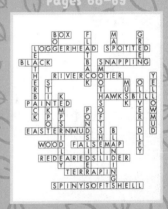

Page 70

Page 72

Page 74

ANSWERS

TAYLOR: Spot, 3rd place
MADISON: Hoppy, 1st place
CAMERON: Freddie, 2nd place

flowers leaves orange	orange brown body	orange dots wings upright
leaves curled antenna	flowers curled antenna dots brown body	curled antenna wings upright
leaves blue dots	blue brown body	flowers blue wings upright

Which sport do insects like better than baseball?

CRICKET

ANSWERS

LETTERS: **A R N T S F**

F	A	S	T	N	R
N	R	T	S	A	F
S	N	A	F	R	T
T	F	R	N	S	A
A	S	F	R	T	N
R	T	N	A	F	S

FRANTS

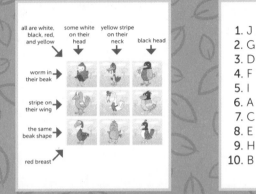

all are white, black, red, and yellow / some white on their head / yellow stripe on their neck / black head

worm in their beak / stripe on their wing / the same beak shape / red breast

1. J
2. G
3. D
4. F
5. I
6. A
7. C
8. E
9. H
10. B

ALLIGATOR
SNAKE
LIZARD
GRASSHOPPER
BEAR
RACCOON
BUTTERFLY
TURTLE
SQUIRREL
ELK

Where do backyard animals keep their food?

IN A PANTREE

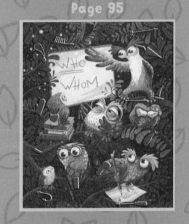

BEAR
BEAT
BEST
BESS
MESS
MISS
MIST
FIST
FISH

MARY: green jar, 1st place
BARRY: purple jar, 3rd place
JERRY: yellow jar, 2nd place

BALL
BUTTON
YARN
RING
PENNY
WHEEL
SUN
CLOCK

ANSWERS

Page 100

Page 103

How do you stop a
skunk from smelling?
YOU HOLD ITS NOSE.

Pages 104–105

Page 106

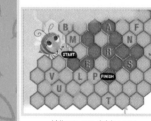

Page 108

What kind of haircut
does a bee get?
IT GETS A *BUZZ* CUT.

Page 109

What would bears
be without bees?
EARS

Page 110

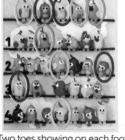

1. Two toes showing on each foot.
2. Spot on belly.
3. Looking up (and closed beaks).
4. Have tan beaks.

Page 114

Page 116

ANSWERS

Page 117

1. T
2. F
3. F
4. T
5. F
6. T
7. T
8. F
9. T
10. F

Page 118

Page 119

Page 120

Page 122

Page 124

X	1	0	X
	X	X	X
3		2	
	2	X	1

		1	X		1
4	X	X	X	X	X
		2	X	X	2
4	X	3			
		2	X	3	X
2	X	X	X	O	X

Page 125

BIRD
BIND
BAND
WAND
WANT
WART
WARM
WORM

Page 127

What do you call a fish with no eyes?

A fish

143

ANSWERS

Pages 128–129

Page 132

Knock, knock.
Who's there?
Owl.
Owl who?
I'm owl out of
animal jokes!

For information about permission to reprint selections from
this book, please contact permissions@highlights.com.

Published by Highlights Press
815 Church Street
Honesdale, Pennsylvania 18431
ISBN: 978-1-64472-680-8
Manufactured in Mattoon, IL, USA
Mfg. 01/2022

First edition
Visit our website at Highlights.com.
10 9 8 7 6 5 4 3 2 1